THE SECRET LIVES OF INSECTS

Corpses, Cats & Mouldy Cheese

The Places Insects Live

by Ruth Owen and Ross Piper

Published in 2018 by Ruby Tuesday Books Ltd.

Editor: Mark J. Sachner
Designer: Emma Randall
Production: John Lingham

Photo credits
Alamy: 5 (top), 22, 28; Creative Commons: 1, 8, 9, 10 (bottom), 11, 15 (bottom), 19, 23 (top), 31; FLPA: 6 (top), 16, 20, 25, 29; Getty Images: 12, 23 (bottom); Istock Photo: 27 (centre); Nature Picture Library: 21, 26; Science Photo Library: Cover; Shutterstock: Cover, 4, 5 (centre), 5 (bottom), 6 (bottom), 7, 10 (top), 13, 14, 15 (top), 17, 18, 24, 27 (top), 27 (bottom).

British Library Cataloguing in Publication Data (CIP) is available for this title.

ISBN 978-1-78856-000-9

Printed in Poland by L&C Printing Group

www.rubytuesdaybooks.com

Words shown in **bold** in the text are explained in the glossary.

Contents

The Places Insects Live..................................4

Tiny, Blood-sucking Lodgers
Cat Flea...6

Their Home, Your Hair!
Head Louse...8

Living in Rotting Cheese
Cheese Fly..10

Living on a Rotting Corpse
Blue Bottle Fly....................................12

A Home Carved from Wood
Bark Beetle...14

Digging a Home
Mole Cricket.......................................16

A Home Under Attack!
Whistling Thorn Ant............................18

A Nest of Leaves and Silk
Weaver Ant...20

A Muddy Nest
Black and Yellow Mud Dauber...............22

Super Builders
Mound-Building Termite........................24

A Home on the Move
Caddisfly..26

A Living Nest
Army Ant..28

Glossary..30

Index, Learn More Online.......................32

The Places Insects Live

Insects are living all around us. Some make their homes in our gardens, living on plants or in the ground beneath our feet. Some of these tiny creatures share our homes, while others actually live . . . well . . . on us!

Some insects build complicated nests that are home to thousands or even millions of family members. Others only build a nest as a safe home for their eggs and young.

Inside this book, we'll see up-close how some of Earth's tiniest animals create a place to call home.

Let's discover the secret world of insect homes. . . .

Check in to a Bug Hotel

If you've ever seen something like the structure in this photo, you've seen a bug hotel. People build bug hotels in parks and gardens to create a place where some insects can raise their young or spend the winter.

A bug hotel

A Place for the Winter

In summer we see ladybirds on leaves and flowers. In winter, these popular insects huddle together in warm, dry hiding places to wait for spring.

Ladybirds inside the dry, hollow stems of a plant.

A paper wasp nest

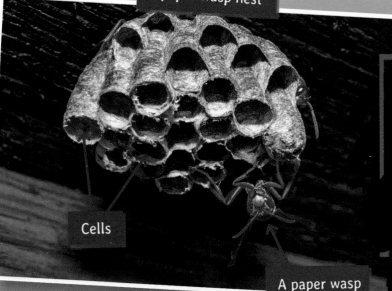

Cells

A Nest Made of Paper

Paper wasps build their nests from paper made of chewed-up plants and spit. The umbrella-like nest has many tiny cells. Each of the cells contains an egg.

A paper wasp

The Science Stuff—What Is an Insect?

- Insects are tiny animals with a body made of three main parts.

- Insects use their antennae to do different things, such as touching, smelling or detecting sounds.

- An insect has a tough outer covering called an exoskeleton.

Antennae

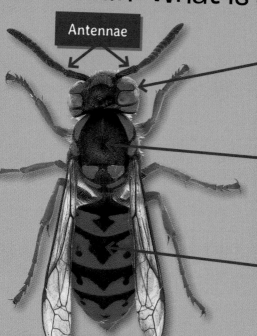

The head contains an insect's brain, eyes, mouthparts and a pair of antennae.

The thorax has six jointed legs and the insect's wings.

The abdomen contains an insect's digestive system and reproductive parts.

5

Tiny, Blood-sucking Lodgers

If you share your home with a cat, it's possible that one day some tiny, blood-sucking lodgers will move in — cat fleas!

At first, a flea makes itself at home on your pet's body. Kitty isn't just a cosy place to live, though. Your cat is a source of food for the hungry invader.

The flea sucks a blowout meal of blood from your cat with its sharp mouthparts. Then the insect hops off Kitty and lives in your pet's bed or in a rug until it needs its next bloody meal.

Cat flea

Powerful back legs for jumping and running

A cat flea's body is actually flat to help it move through the hairs of a cat's thick coat.

The Science Stuff
A Cat Flea's Life Cycle

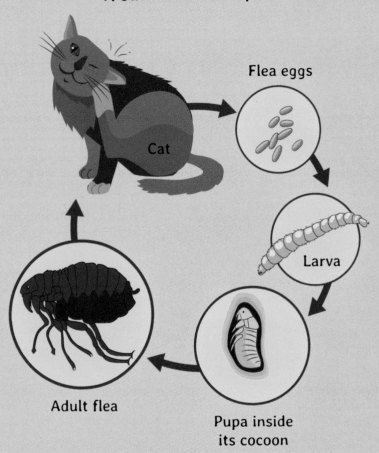

Cat

Flea eggs

Larva

Pupa inside its cocoon

Adult flea

Once a female cat flea has mated and drunk a meal of blood, she lays eggs.

The flea usually lays her eggs on furniture, in carpets and in your pet's bed.

A tiny, worm-like **larva** hatches from each egg.

Within two weeks, the larva becomes a **pupa**. It spins a **cocoon** of sticky silk from its own body. Inside the cocoon, it becomes an adult flea.

The flea waits inside its cocoon until it feels warmth or vibrations. Then it knows that Kitty is nearby. The new flea emerges from the cocoon and hops onto your pet for a meal.

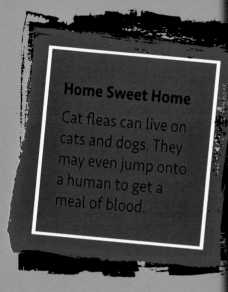

Home Sweet Home
Cat fleas can live on cats and dogs. They may even jump onto a human to get a meal of blood.

What Do Baby Fleas Eat?
A flea larva eats flakes of skin and pet hair. It also feeds on flea dirt, which is the dry, bloody poo of adult fleas!

Their Home, Your Hair!

Feeling itchy yet? You soon will be. . . .

This next insect's name tells you exactly where it makes its home. The speck-like head louse lives on a head — a human head!

Safely snuggled in a person's hair, this tiny bloodsucker pierces the skin of its human **host** with its mouthparts. Then it feeds on blood, up to four times a day. These **parasites** don't only suck blood, they can also reproduce quickly. Within weeks, a person's head can be home to **generations** of little bloodsuckers.

Blood that the head louse has sucked from its host.

Head lice aren't fussy. They will live in clean hair and dirty hair.

A head louse has strong legs and large claws for holding onto hairs.

An adult head louse

The Science Stuff

A head louse lives for about a month.

In that time, a female louse may lay up to 150 eggs.

Using glue from her body, she sticks each egg to a single hair.

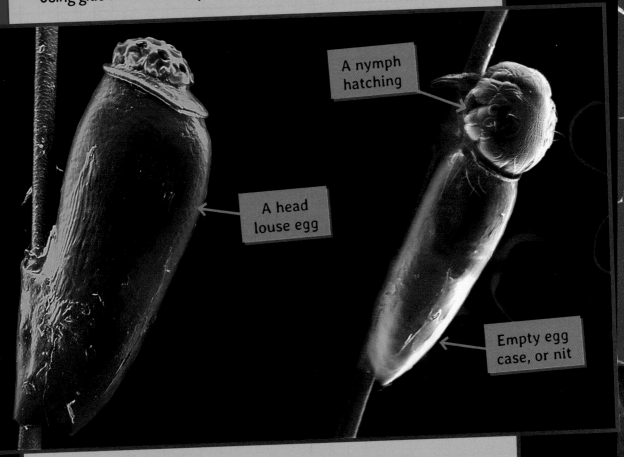

A nymph hatching

A head louse egg

Empty egg case, or nit

A young louse, called a **nymph**, hatches from an egg.

A nymph grows and becomes an adult that is ready to reproduce in just two weeks.

Sticky Nits

People sometimes call head lice nits. A nit is actually the empty egg case that's left stuck to a hair once a nymph hatches.

A New Home

A head louse can move home by crawling from one person's head to another. It might also swing from hair to hair — just like a tiny, blood-sucking Tarzan!

Living in Rotting Cheese

When you're a cheese fly larva, or maggot, the perfect place to live is inside a rotting chunk of Casu Marzu cheese.

Pecorino cheese

Casu Marzu comes from the Italian island of Sardinia. To make this horrifying **delicacy**, some rind is cut from a pecorino cheese. This allows female cheese flies to crawl into the pecorino and lay their eggs.

When maggots hatch from the eggs, they start eating their cheesy home. As the maggots feed, the cheese begins to **decompose**. Once it becomes soft and runny, the cheese is ready to eat — by people!

Pecorino cheese is made from sheep's milk.

A block of Casu Marzu may be home to thousands of wriggling maggots.

In English, Casu Marzu means "rotten cheese".

A cheese fly

A cheese fly may lay up to 500 eggs at one time.

There's a Maggot in My Sandwich!

Casu Marzu fans eat the rotting cheese spread on bread. Sometimes they remove the maggots before eating . . . and sometimes they don't!

The Science Stuff

As cheese fly maggots feed on the pecorino cheese, digestive juices from their bodies leak onto the cheese. The juices start to break down the fats in the cheese and make it start to rot.

Cheese fly maggots

Rotting Casu Marzu cheese

Illegal Cheese

Casu Marzu has been around for many years. The maggoty cheese is now illegal because it could make a person very ill. However, some people break the law and still enjoy their rotting snack.

A cheese fly larva is about the size of a grain of rice.

Living on a Rotting Corpse

When it's time for a female blue bottle fly to lay her eggs, she goes in search of the perfect home for her young — a fresh **corpse!**

Flesh

A single blue bottle can lay more than 500 eggs on a dead body. In less than 48 hours, hundreds of tiny white larvae, or maggots, hatch from the eggs.

The young flies immediately start feeding on their juicy, rotting home. They crawl over the dead body and often **burrow** down into the meat to feed.

A blue bottle maggot

An adult blue bottle fly

These flies get their name from their shiny blue abdomens.

The Science Stuff

If you happen to discover a dead bird or other animal covered with maggots, it may look disgusting. However, the young insects are actually very helpful. As they feed, maggots help break down dead bodies.

Along with **fungi**, **bacteria** and other insects, fly maggots are nature's clean-up crew. Without them, our world would quickly become littered with stinky, rotting dead bodies and plants.

Dead rat

Maggots

A Blue Bottle's Life Cycle

After about a week of feasting, a blue bottle maggot buries itself in dry soil. It becomes a pupa with a hard, brownish-red shell called a puparium. About two weeks later, the insect emerges from its puparium as an adult fly.

Blowflies

A dead body usually inflates, or blows up, with gases. Blue bottles are sometimes called blowflies because they visit blown corpses to lay eggs.

A Home Carved from Wood

Bark beetles make their homes in trees.

When a male bark beetle is ready to mate, he chews his way under the bark of a tree. In the soft wood beneath the bark, he makes a small chamber, or room. Then he releases chemicals, called **pheromones**, to tell female beetles to come to the tree to mate with him.

After mating, the female beetles make tunnels that lead from the male's chamber. The females lay their eggs in the tunnels. Once larvae hatch from the eggs, the larvae also start chewing and making tiny tunnels in the wood.

Tunnels made by bark beetles

Engraver Beetles

Bark beetles are also known as engraver beetles. This is because their homes look as if a person has engraved, or carved, a pattern in the wood.

Tiny Munchers

Bark beetles make chambers and tunnels in a tree by chewing the wood with their strong mouthparts.

An adult bark beetle is smaller than a grain of rice.

The Science Stuff

Some bark beetles and their larvae feed on the part of a tree called the phloem (FLOH-em).

Phloem is the **tissue** that carries food made by the leaves throughout a tree.

The beetles eat the sugary food made by the tree.

A Bark Beetle Grows Up

After a bark beetle larva **pupates** and becomes an adult, it flies from its home. Then it finds a new tree where it can mate and have a family of its own.

A bark beetle larva

Digging a Home

Mole crickets are insects that dig burrows
in lawns, fields and other grassy places.

A mole cricket digs a tiny entrance hole to its burrow that's
about the size of a penny. Then it digs short tunnels, called
galleries, just below the ground. It also digs tunnels that are
deeper below the surface.

By day, a mole cricket rests in its deep tunnels. At night, it
moves closer to the surface. It crawls through the network of
galleries searching for roots, other insects and worms to eat.

A mole cricket is about
5 centimetres long.

Burrow

Mole
cricket

Claws

Built for Digging

A mole cricket has long claws for digging on its front legs. It uses its strong front legs to scoop up soil and push it aside.

How the Mole Cricket Got Its Name

There are thousands of **species** of crickets. Mole crickets got their name because they have claws like moles and they dig underground homes.

The Science Stuff

To attract a female, a male mole cricket rubs his wings together. This makes fast, buzzing sounds called trills.

Some types of male mole crickets shape the entrances to their burrows like a trumpet. They sit in the entrance and make trilling noises. The trumpet-like shape of the burrow makes the trills much louder.

When a female cricket hears the trills, she flies to the burrow to mate with the male. After mating, she digs a tiny round room in the male's burrow, where she lays her eggs.

A mole

A Home Under Attack!

On the hot, dry African savanna stands a whistling acacia tree.

An elephant comes close to pick itself some leaves and twigs to eat. The tree's branches are covered with long, sharp thorns to keep hungry plant-eaters at bay. However, the sensitive tip of the elephant's trunk is able to easily avoid the thorns.

Ouch, ouch, ouch! Suddenly the tip of the elephant's trunk is under attack by an army of angry, stinging ants. The tree is the ants' home, and the tiny insects are not about to let a giant thief help itself to their supply of juicy leaves!

A whistling acacia tree

The Science Stuff

The thorns of a whistling acacia tree have swollen, hollow bases. Ants make their homes in the round bases of the thorns.

Each rounded base has tiny entrance and exit holes that are used by the ants. When the wind blows through these holes, it makes a whistling sound that gives the trees their name.

Ants on the thorns of a whistling acacia tree

Acacia thorn

Swollen base of thorn

A Home and a Food Supply

Whistling thorn ants feed on sugary **nectar** that's produced by special parts of the acacia tree's leaves.

A Nest of Leaves and Silk

For a **colony** of weaver ants, building nests is a family affair. Even the baby ants, or larvae, have work to do!

Worker ants pulling leaf edges together

To build a nest, a row of worker ants lines up on the edge of a leaf. Then the workers grab another leaf edge and pull the two together.

Next, ant larvae are carried to the leaf edges by worker ants. The larvae produce silk from their heads that is used to stitch the leaf edges together.

Like making a patchwork quilt, the ants continue to stitch together leaves until they have created their home.

Worker

Larva

Silk

Weaver ants build their nests at night.

Weaver ants are also known as green ants.

A weaver ant nest

Silk

The Science Stuff

A weaver ant colony can have about 500,000 members. The colony may build several nests in a single tree or have nests in more than one tree.

The queen ant lives in one of the nests. Her job is to lay eggs. The other nests are home to the colony's larvae and workers.

Worker weaver ants

A Muddy Nest

After mating, a female black and yellow mud dauber wasp builds a cosy home for her young — from mud!

The female wasp gathers tiny balls of mud and carries them to her nest site. She uses the mud to build a tiny room, or cell. Inside the cell, she lays a single egg. She also places food in the cell for her larva to eat once it hatches.

In total, the mother wasp builds about 25 cells and lays an egg in each one. Then she covers the cells with mud to join them together.

A female mud dauber wasp

Ball of mud for building

A mud dauber wasp collects mud from the edges of muddy puddles and small pools.

Two cells joined together with mud

Mud daubers often build their nests on houses or other buildings.

The Science Stuff

After a female mud dauber has built a cell, she goes hunting for spiders. She stings the spiders so they are **paralyzed** and cannot escape.

She places about 25 spiders inside each cell alongside her egg. Then she plugs up the cell with more mud.

When a larva hatches, it feeds on live spiders until it is ready to pupate and become an adult.

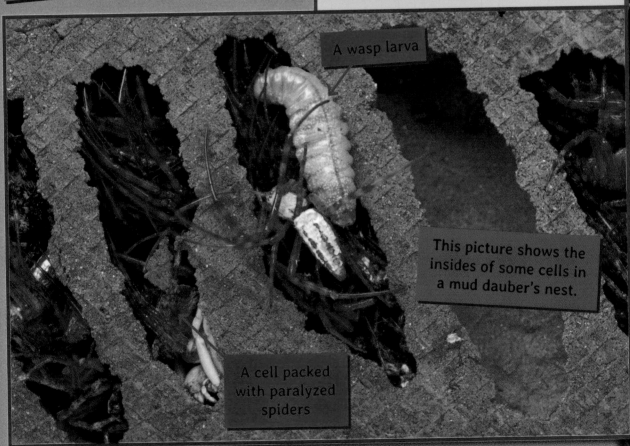

A wasp larva

This picture shows the insides of some cells in a mud dauber's nest.

A cell packed with paralyzed spiders

Fresh Food

A mud dauber paralyzes the spiders she catches so they are still alive. This keeps them fresher for her larvae to eat!

Super Builders

Take a million mini builders and plenty of mud, and what do you get? A magnificent termite home that can be 9 metres high!

The rock-hard mound is made of mud, termite spit and chewed-up plants.

A termite mound

Termites build the mound by placing billions of tiny mouthfuls of mud one on top of the next.

The mound is designed to help the termites breathe, stop the nest drying out and keep the nest at just the right temperature.

The termite colony actually lives below ground in a network of chambers and tunnels.

The Science Stuff

Scientists have discovered that a termite mound works a little like a giant set of lungs.

The mound contains chambers and passages. As air flows through the mound, unwanted carbon dioxide is pushed out and oxygen that's needed by the termites is sucked in.

The mound looks solid, but gases are actually able to pass through its muddy walls.

When termites construct a mound, they have no instructions and no chief engineer giving them orders. Scientists have yet to discover how each termite knows exactly what to do.

Meet the Family

A termite colony includes a queen who lays hundreds of eggs each day. It also includes soldier termites and workers who build the mound, find food and care for the queen, her eggs and larvae.

A queen termite

Workers caring for the queen

Soldier termites guarding a hole

The Emergency Crew

If the mound is damaged, soldiers rush to guard any holes or breaks against intruders. Then workers with mouthfuls of dirt quickly arrive to patch up the damage.

A Home on the Move

Why build a home that's attached to one place when you can build a mobile home that goes everywhere you go? This is exactly what a case-building caddisfly larva does.

Case

Larvae

A female case-building caddisfly lays her eggs on a plant overhanging a stream, river or pond. Once a larva hatches, it drops into the water. The larva quickly spins a case of silk around its body. Next, the larva attaches other materials, such as grains of sand, to the silk case, making itself a **portable**, protective home.

Too Hard To Eat

A caddisfly larva's case helps it to blend in with its environment and stay hidden from fish and other **predators**. A tough outer case of pebbles also makes the little insect a less-than-inviting snack!

A case made from pebbles

A case made from strips of plants

Larva

The Science Stuff

Different species of caddisfly use different building materials. Pebbles, leaves, empty shells and seeds are all used by caddisfly larvae to build their homes.

An adult caddisfly

All Grown Up

When it's ready to grow up, a caddisfly larva pupates inside its case. When it emerges as an adult, it can fly and no longer lives underwater or builds a case.

A Living Nest

Army ants are constantly on the move, so it makes no sense to build a permanent home.

These tiny but fierce hunters feed on any small creature they can catch. Once a colony has eaten all the **prey** in an area, it marches on.

When it's time for the colony to rest in one spot, the ants create a living nest with their bodies. The queen ant, eggs and larvae are safe in the centre of the nest. Then hundreds of thousands of colony members surround them, clinging together.

The hooks on an army ant's foot

The Science Stuff

When creating a nest, each ant connects to its neighbour with its hooked feet.

An Army Camp

The living nest formed from ants is called a bivouac. The ants may build their bivouac inside a hollow log or empty animal burrow. The nest might also be hung from a tree.

An army ant colony may have 2 million members.

The ants in this photo have just started building a new nest.

Safety in Numbers

If a predator comes too near to the army ant nest, it better be ready to get bitten and stung — thousands of times!

bacteria
Microscopic living things. Some bacteria are helpful, while others can cause disease.

burrow
The action of digging or burrowing into something. Also a hole or tunnel in the ground dug by an animal as a home.

cocoon
A protective case made by some insect larvae. A larva pupates inside its cocoon.

colony
A large group of insects that live together and work together to find food, raise young and protect each other.

corpse
A dead body.

decompose
To rot.

delicacy
A special or unusual food.

fungus
A living thing from a group that includes mushrooms, toadstools and moulds.

generation
A group of animals or people born around the same time.

host
A living plant or animal from which a parasite gets its food.

larva
The young form of some animals, including insects, fish and frogs.

nectar
A sugary liquid produced by plants.

nymph
The young form of some insects, between an egg and adult.

paralyze
To make unable to move.

parasite
A living thing that spends part or all of its life living and feeding on another living thing.

pheromone
A chemical released by an animal that affects the behaviour of other animals, usually of the same species. For example, an animal might release pheromones to attract a mate.

portable
Able to be carried.

predator
An animal that hunts and eats other animals.

prey
An animal that is hunted by other animals for food.

pupa
A stage in the life cycle of some insects between being a larva and becoming an adult.

pupation
Changing from a larva to an adult insect.

species
Different types of living things. The members of an animal species look alike and can produce young together.

tissue
A group of connected cells that work together to do a particular job inside a plant or in the body of an animal.

Millions of Insects

Scientists have identified about one million different insect species. There are millions more yet to be discovered, identified and studied.

A

army ants 28—29

B

bark beetles 14—15
black and yellow mud
    daubers 22—23
blue bottle flies 12—13

C

caddisflies 26—27
cat fleas 6—7
cats 6—7
cheese 10—11
cheese flies 10—11
corpses 12—13

E

eggs 4—5, 7, 9, 10—11,
    12—13, 14, 17, 21,
    22—23, 25, 26, 28

H

head lice 8—9

L

ladybirds 5
larvae 7, 10—11, 12—13,
    14—15, 20—21,
    22—23, 25, 26—27, 28

M

maggots 10—11, 12—13
mole crickets 16—17
mound-building
    termites 24—25

N

nymphs 9

P

paper wasps 5

W

weaver ants 20—21
whistling thorn ants
    18—19

LEARN MORE ONLINE

To learn more about where insects live, go to:
www.rubytuesdaybooks.com/insects